A family can mean the one
we were born into, or one we've
chosen. It may be made up of
relatives, or loyal friends. It may
be linked by lineage—or by love alone.
Most of us have some of both kinds
of family in our lives.

Families today are varied
and wonderful.

This little book is a warm
reminder of the good feelings a
sense of family can bring.

A Family Is
A Circle Of People
Who Love You

• Doris Jasinek and Pamela Bell Ryan •

Illustrated by Caroline Price

CompCare®
Publishers

Jasinek, Doris.
     A family is a circle of people who love you/Doris Jasinek and Pamela
Bell Ryan.
          p.   cm.
     ISBN 0-89638-153-6
     1. Family.   I. Ryan, Pamela Bell.   II. Title.
     HQ518.J37 1988   88-19855
     306.8'5—dc19   CIP

Illustrations by Caroline Price
Cover and interior design by MacLean & Tuminelly

Inquiries, orders, and catalog requests should be addressed to
CompCare Publishers
2415 Annapolis Lane
Minneapolis, Minnesota 55441
Call toll free 800/328-3330
Minnesota residents 612/559-4800

6   5   4   3   2
93   92   91   90   89   88

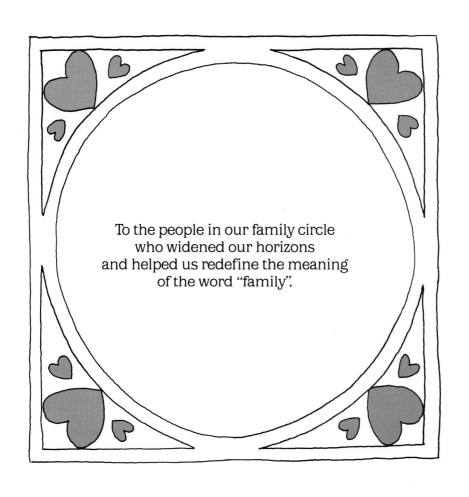

To the people in our family circle
who widened our horizons
and helped us redefine the meaning
of the word "family".

A family is a place to begin and a place to belong.

What's your idea of
what a family can be?

It may be the typical
Mom-Dad-kids-dog-cat family.

Or it may be a family lovingly
selected from the special people
you know.

A family is a circle of people
who love you.

Add a newcomer to your circle.

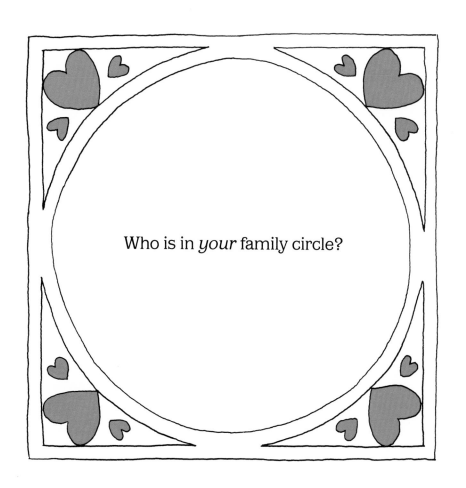

Who is in *your* family circle?

One parent?
Two parents?
No parents?

One child?
Ten children?
No children?

One grandparent?
Four grandparents?
Or more?

Add an extra grandparent to your family circle.

Is your family linked by lineage?

Or by love alone?

A family may be related...

unrelated…

...or belated.

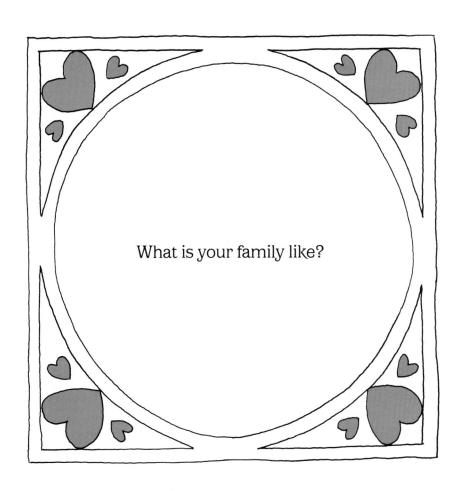

What is your family like?

Some families
are conservative.

Some are liberal.

Some are purple.

Add someone with a fresh point of view to your circle.

Is your family quiet?
Or loud?

Love can speak in whispers.
Love can yell.

Is your family
in the next room?

Or in the next country?

Love travels well.

Love hurdles walls.

Love crosses cultures.

Is your circle fractured?

Is it mended,
blended…

...or extended?

Love can be rekindled.
The capacity to love withstands heartbreak.

Is your family huggy?

Or stuffy?

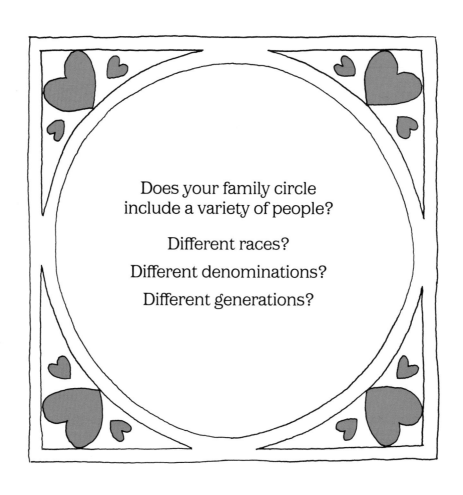

Does your family circle
include a variety of people?

Different races?

Different denominations?

Different generations?

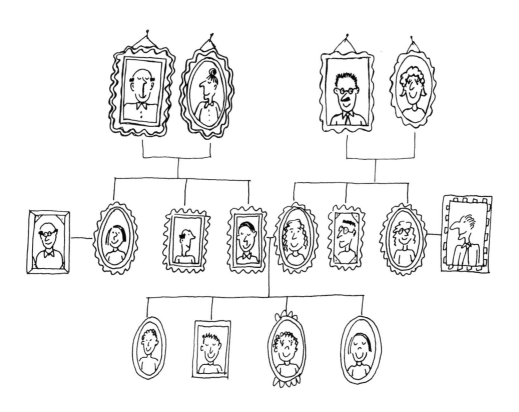

Your family circle may build slowly
with the seasons of time ...

...or it can grow by leaps and bounds.

Let someone dance into your family.

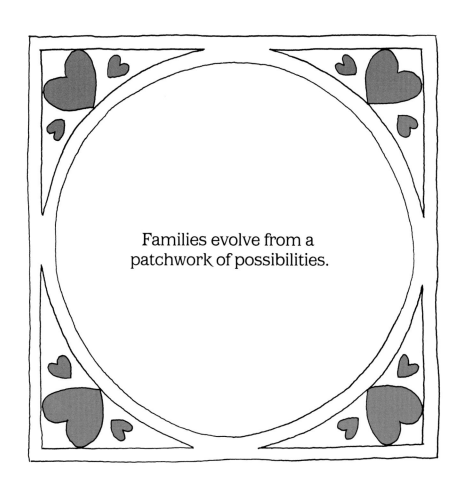

Families evolve from a
patchwork of possibilities.

They can be intimate relations…

reluctant relatives...

...or plagues of relatives.

Add a shirttail relative to your family circle.

A family may be made up of
lifelong friends…

or the girls,
the boys,
the gang,
the team.

Add a new team member to your family circle.

You might find family among the flight crew…

the pit crew…

...the rowing crew.

Is it time to get somebody new on board?

Maybe family begins with the herd...

the flock…

...the gaggle.

Welcome some stragglers from the gaggle.

Your family might be the people
in your neighborhood...

your health club, your bird club,
your car pool, or your support group.

Your family is anywhere
you want or need one.
You carry your family spirit
within you.

Family is a frame of mind.

To keep the people in your life,
nurture them!

Laugh.
Kiss.
Reminisce.

Get involved with them!

Cooperate.
Participate.
Negotiate.

Communicate with them!

Phone.
Write.
Unite.

Do nice things for them!

Know when they need a friend.
Call them just to touch base.

Encourage them!

Let them hear:
"Go for it!"
"Try again!"
"I knew you could do it!"

Enjoy them!

Eat.
Link.
And be merry.

Hug!

Hug!

Hug!

The family spirit is endangered.

Protect it.

Now what's your idea
of what a family can be?

You may have discovered that
you have more family
than you thought.

Explore.
Reach out.

Imagine yourself a family—
and make your family come true.

No one is without a family—
except those who haven't yet
opened their hearts.

A heart that gives
gathers family.

About the authors

Doris Jasinek has spent twenty years as a teacher, administrator, camp director, consultant, and lecturer. For fourteen years she has been director of Bethlehem Community Preschool in Encinitas, California.

She studied at University of California in San Diego, San Diego State University, and University of London, where she learned about British infant schools. She has two grown children and three grandchildren.

Pamela Bell Ryan is a graduate of Bakersfield Junior College and San Diego State University, where she is now working toward a master's degree in education. She has been involved in early childhood education as a bilingual teacher, assistant director, and volunteer coordinator for Red Cross refugee playschools.

She is editor of the Encinitas library's newsletter, *The Friend Ship,* written by and for elementary school children. She and Doris serve on a committee for the Bethlehem Lutheran Church Expansion Project, which will encompass a community care center for children and seniors.

She and her husband, Jim, live in Leucadia, California. Their lively household also includes daughters aged eleven and seven, and twin five-year-old boys.

The same authors wrote *How to Build a House of Hearts* (CompCare Publishers), about living in a family and communicating at heart level.

About the illustrator

Caroline Price—whose drawings add charm and whimsy to this little book about open-ended, open-hearted families—lives in Minneapolis. She earned a degree in art history from Colorado College and studied at University of Pennsylvania and Minneapolis College of Art and Design. She has illustrated several books, including *How to Build a House of Hearts*, also by Doris Jasinek and Pamela Bell Ryan.